King of The Jews

Written and Illustrated

by

Pauline Shone

Olive Shoots
Imprint of

Publisher

King of The Jews

Written and Illustrated
by
Pauline Shone

King of the Jews

"Feed My Sheep" Series

Written and Illustrated by Pauline Shone

Copyright © 2008, 2025 by Pauline Shone, Simon Books, Derbyshire, England,

ISBN: 978-0-9557729-1-7

All rights reserved. No part of this book may be reproduced or transmitted in any form or by any means—electronic, mechanical, photocopying, or any information stored in a retrievable system,—without the prior permission of the copyright holder, according to USA and UK copyright laws.

Published by

Olive Shoots

an Imprint of:

Olive Press Publisher

www.olivepresspublisher.com

olivepressbooks@gmail.com

All Scripture quotes are taken from the *Holy Bible, New Living Translation*, copyright © 1996, 2004, 2015 by Tyndale House Foundation. Used by permission of Tyndale House Publishers, Inc., Carol Stream, Illinois 60188. All rights reserved.

All pronouns referring to the Trinity are capitalized.

FOREWORD

In biblical times, only rich and powerful people owned horses. In times of war, horses and chariots were an important part of an army. But the common donkey was used for carrying heavy loads, and also for riding by rich and poor alike.

Yet Jesus, the King of the Jews, rode into Jerusalem on the unbroken colt of a donkey.

As it is written:

*"Rejoice, O people of Zion!
Shout in triumph, O people
of Jerusalem!
Look, your King is coming to you.
He is righteous and victorious,
yet He is humble, riding on a donkey,
riding on a donkey's colt."*

Zechariah 9:9

The Death of Lazarus

Lazarus lived with his two sisters, Martha and Mary. Their home was in the village of Bethany in Judea. Now Lazarus was a dear friend of Jesus. So when he was sick, his sisters sent a message to Jesus.

Yet when He heard the news, Jesus stayed where He was for two more days! Then He told His disciples that Lazarus had fallen asleep and He was going to wake him up. But they said Jesus had many enemies in Judea. If Lazarus was sleeping, he would soon get better! But Jesus meant that Lazarus had died.

When Jesus and His disciples finally arrived in Bethany, Lazarus had already been in his grave for four days. Bethany was near Jerusalem, so many Jews had come to comfort Martha and Mary. As soon as Martha heard that Jesus was coming, she went out to meet Him. But Mary stayed at home.

Martha said to Jesus, "Lord, if only You had been here, my brother would not have died. But even now I know that God will give you whatever you ask." John 11:21-22

The Son of God

Jesus told her, "I am the resurrection and the life. Anyone who believes in Me will live, even after dying. Everyone who lives in Me and believes in Me will never ever die. Do you believe this Martha?"   John 11:25-26

And Martha said she had always believed He was the Messiah, the Son of God.

Then Martha hurried home to tell Mary that the Teacher was here. When Mary heard that Jesus wanted to see her, she quickly left the house. Now the mourners in the house thought she was going to her brother's grave to weep, so they followed. But Mary went to meet Jesus outside the village. When she saw Him, she fell weeping at his feet. If only He had come earlier, then her brother would not have died!

Seeing Mary and the people with her weeping, Jesus was deeply troubled. He asked where they had put Lazarus' body, and they led Him to the tomb. Then Jesus also began to weep, and everyone realised how much He had loved Lazarus. But others said that this Man had healed a blind man. Couldn't He have kept Lazarus from dying?

Lazarus is Raised from the Dead!

Jesus stood before the cave where Lazarus was laid. Then He told them to roll away the stone covering the entrance. Well, everyone was shocked at His words, and Martha protested that her brother had been dead for four days! She said the stench of decay would be terrible! But Jesus reminded Martha of His promise. If she believed, she would see God's glory. So they rolled away the stone.

Then Jesus looked up to heaven and said, "Father, thank You for hearing Me. You always hear Me, but I said it out loud for the sake of all these people standing here, so that they will believe You sent Me." Then Jesus shouted, "Lazarus, come out!"
John 11:40-43

And Lazarus came out, still bound hand and foot with grave clothes! Jesus told them to unloose the strips of linen and let him go.

The Plot to Kill Jesus

After seeing this great miracle, many of the Jews with Mary believed in Jesus. But some went to the Pharisees and told them what Jesus had done. Then all the leading priests and Pharisees called a meeting of the council, to decide what to do. It was true that Jesus was working many mighty miracles. If He wasn't stopped, everyone would believe in Him, and then they would lose their positions of authority!

Caiaphas, who was high priest at that time, said, "You don't know what you're talking about! You don't realise that it's better for you that one man should die for the people than for the whole nation to be destroyed." John 11:49-50

But Caiaphas was not speaking his own thoughts. As high priest that year, he was giving a message from God. Saying that Jesus was going to die for the nation of Israel, and for the Gentiles as well.

From that day on, the Jewish leaders began to plot Jesus' death. So Jesus no longer went out freely among the people. He withdrew to a place near the desert and stayed in the village of Ephraim with His disciples.

Now the Jewish Passover was near. And many Jews had travelled up to Jerusalem early, so they could purify themselves before the Passover ceremony. (It was the custom, to wash their bodies and clothing before entering the Temple to worship).

And some of these Jews were hoping to see Jesus in Jerusalem. But the chief priests and Pharisees gave orders that anyone who saw Him must report it, so they could arrest Him.

Jerusalem

Crowds of Jews with their baggage and donkeys were travelling up from the country to Jerusalem. And many of them were talking about Jesus' latest miracle. Surely He was the Messiah, if He had raised Lazarus of Bethany from the dead!

Jesus and His disciples were also going to celebrate the Passover in Jerusalem. But Jesus warned His disciples that He would be arrested there. The chief priests and teachers of the law would condemn Him to death and hand Him over to the Romans to be crucified.

But His disciples didn't understand what Jesus was talking about. He was their Messiah and the King of Israel who the people had been waiting for! But after Jesus' death, they would remember His warning and understand.

It was sometimes hard for the followers of Jesus to understand Him. Jesus' way of thinking and acting was so very different from their own! One time, the mother of His disciples, James and John, asked Jesus if her sons could sit in places of honour with Him in His kingdom. And when the other disciples heard her request they were very angry!

Then Jesus patiently explained that leaders of earthly kingdoms ruled with selfish pride. But Jesus' kingdom was not of this world and His disciples must act like servants. Even though He Himself was the Son of God, He had come to serve the people and to give His life as a ransom for many.

Mary Anoints Jesus at Bethany

Six days before Passover, Jesus arrived in Bethany and went to the home of His friend Lazarus. That evening they invited Him to eat with them. So while Martha was serving the food, Lazarus and the other guests ate at the table with Jesus.

Then Mary took a jar of expensive spikenard perfume, poured it over Jesus' feet, and wiped His feet with her hair. The house was filled with the beautiful perfume. But Judas complained.

"That perfume was worth a year's wages. It should have been sold and the money given to the poor."

John 12:5

But Judas did not care at all about the poor. He said this because he was a thief. He was in charge of the disciples' money box and often stole from it! Jesus replied, "Leave her alone. She did this in preparation for My burial. You will always have the poor among you, but you will not always have Me"

John 12: 7-8

When the Jewish people heard that Jesus was there, many came to see Him and the man He had raised from the dead. Then the chief priests decided to kill Lazarus too. For It was because of him that many of the people believed in Jesus.

Four Days Before Passover

Four days before Passover, was a time when every Jewish family chose a lamb. Then the night before Passover it was killed and the roasted meat was part of the celebration meal. And during this special meal, families would tell the story of how God had rescued their ancestors from slavery in Egypt.

God had commanded Pharaoh to let His people go, but the proud king of Egypt had refused. And even though God sent plagues upon Egypt, the stubborn king would not obey Him. Finally, God told Pharaoh that His tenth plague would kill every firstborn in the land. Yet the foolish king even ignored this terrible warning!

To protect His people from the plague on Egypt, God told Moses that each family had to take a lamb. Then in the evening before the final plague, the lambs were to be killed and some of the blood smeared on the doorposts and lintels of their houses. And that night His people should all stay in their homes.

At midnight, God would go through Egypt and strike dead every firstborn in the land. But wherever He saw the blood, He would "pass over" those homes. So the people inside were not harmed. Now after Egypt's devastating and terrible punishment, Pharaoh let God's people go. Then they began their journey to the Promised Land.

Son of David

News had spread quickly through Jerusalem that Jesus was on His way to the city. And many people cut palm branches as they made their way to meet Him, and they began to shout.

> "Praise God!
> Blessings on the One who comes in
> the name of the LORD!!
> Hail to the King of Israel!"
> John 12:13

Meanwhile, Jesus had told His disciples to go into the village ahead of them and they would see a donkey with its colt. They must untie these two donkeys and bring them to Him. And if anyone asked what they were doing, they should say that the Lord needed them.

So the disciples did as Jesus asked and brought the donkeys to Him. Then they threw their cloaks over the colt and Jesus sat on him. Just as the Scriptures said He would!

"Don't be afraid, people of Jerusalem.
Look, your King is coming,
riding on a donkey's colt."

Zechariah 9:9 and John 12:15

Jesus in the Temple

After entering the city, Jesus went to the Temple and angrily drove out the people buying and selling animals for sacrifice. Then He overturned the money changers tables, and the chairs of those selling doves.

He said to them, "The Scriptures declare, 'My Temple will be called a house of prayer,' but you have turned it into a den of thieves!"   Matthew 21:13

Then the blind and lame came to Jesus in the Temple, and He healed them. The chief priests and teachers of the law were annoyed when they saw the wonderful things Jesus was doing and heard the children shouting:

"Praise God for the Son of David."   Matthew 21:15

Jesus asked them if they had never read the Scriptures, saying that God had taught children and infants to give Him praise? (Psalm 8:2)

After this, Jesus left the city. He returned to Bethany and stayed there overnight.

Jesus is Betrayed

Now Judas Ischariot, one of Jesus' twelve disciples, went secretly to the high priests.

He asked, "How much will you pay me to betray Jesus to you?" And they gave him thirty pieces of silver. From that time on, Judas began looking for an opportunity to betray Jesus.   Matthew 26:15-16

The Passover Meal

Jesus' disciples asked Him where they should prepare the Passover meal.

"As you go into the city," he told them, "you will see a certain man. Tell him, 'The Teacher says: My time has come, and I will eat the Passover meal with my disciples at your house.'" So the disciples did as Jesus told them and prepared the Passover meal there. Matthew 26:18-19

Before the Passover supper, Jesus took a towel and a basin filled with water. Then one by one, He tenderly washed His disciples' feet, showing them how to humbly love and serve one another.

The New Covenant

Afterwards, Jesus sat at the table and ate the Passover meal with His disciples. Then He blessed the bread, broke it in pieces, and gave it to His disciples. He said that the unleavened bread symbolised His body.

And after giving thanks to God for the wine, Jesus told each of His disciples to drink it. For this wine symbolised the blood of God's new covenant. His blood, would be poured out for many for the forgiveness of sins.

> "But this is the new covenant I will make with the people of Israel after those days," says the LORD. "I will put my instructions deep within them, and I will write them on their hearts. I will be their God, and they will be My people. And they will not need to teach their neighbours, nor will they need to teach their relatives, saying, 'You should know the LORD.' For everyone, from the least to the greatest, will know Me already," says the LORD. "And I will forgive their wickedness, and I will never again remember their sins."
>
> Jeremiah 31:33-34

Jesus is Betrayed and Arrested

While they were eating, He said, "I tell you the truth, one of you will betray Me."

Greatly distressed, each one asked in turn, "Am I the one, Lord?"

He replied, "One of you who has just eaten from this bowl with me will betray me.
         Matthew 26:21-23

Judas, the one who would betray Him, also asked, "Rabbi, am I the one?"

Jesus told him, "You have said it."
           Matthew 26:25

After supper, Jesus and His disciples went to the olive grove called Gethsemane. Then Jesus asked His disciples to wait while He prayed to His Father. He was deeply troubled. He knew that the time had come for His betrayal, and all that He was going to suffer. Jesus felt crushed by the weight of all that lay ahead. Yet He was still willing to be the sacrificial Passover Lamb, and die for the sins of the whole world.

Now Judas knew that Jesus often went to the Garden of Gethsemane with His disciples. While Jesus was still speaking, Judas arrived with a large group of Roman soldiers and Temple guards carrying torches, lanterns, and weapons.

Jesus knew that they had come to arrest Him, but He did not try to escape. He was willing to go through the suffering that would lead to the salvation of many. So Jesus was arrested, then tied up and led away to the house of the high priest Annas. Peter and John followed behind, but the other disciples fled away.

He was oppressed and treated harshly,
yet He never said a word.
He was led like a lamb to the slaughter.
And as a sheep is silent before the shearers,
He did not open His mouth.
Unjustly condemned,
He was led away.
No one cared that He died without descendants,
that His life was cut short in midstream.
But He was stuck down
for the rebellion of my people.
He had done nothing wrong
and had never deceived anyone.
But He was buried like a criminal;
He was put in a rich man's grave.
Isaiah 53:7-9

Jesus is Alive and Will Come Again!

Everything that Jesus had told His disciples came to pass. He was betrayed in Jerusalem, arrested, and sentenced to death by the chief priests and Pharisees. Then they handed Him over to the Romans to be crucified.

But after three days, God's power raised Him to life! The tomb where He had been laid was empty. Jesus appeared to His disciples and many others. Then He returned to His Father in heaven.

One day, Jesus will come again to earth. And at His second coming, He will be riding on a magnificent white horse. He will fight against all those who hate God. Then, having won the battle, He will rule from His throne in Jerusalem, and reign over the whole earth!

About the Author

God gave British author Pauline Shone a very special gift. It was the gift of creativity. And at seven years old, she made her first illustration, Prince Charming dancing with Cinderella! And at sixteen years of age, she began a five year Art College Degree Course. This led to a career in teaching, and then as a designer and sculptor for the ceramic industry. But after coming to a personal faith in Jesus as her Saviour, she used her God-given gift for Him. Over many years she created two series of illustrated Bible Stories for children.

Books by the Author

Feed My Lambs series, colouring books:

Feed My Sheep series for children ages 8-12
Illustrated Bible story books 8.5 x 11

 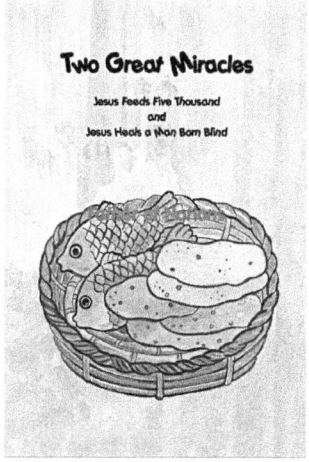 

Illustrated Bible story books 6 x 9

Bible story in full colour hard cover

Bible study book for teens

Adult paperback books

www.ingramcontent.com/pod-product-compliance
Lightning Source LLC
Chambersburg PA
CBHW062106290426
44110CB00022B/2726